Ships and cranes

Peter Firmin

A & C Black · London

Contents

With grateful thanks to the following people who helped to make the
models for this book: Dorian, Lewis, Ruth, Olivia, Sam, Laurence and Oliver.

A CIP catalogue record for this book is available from the British Library.

First published 1994 by A & C Black (Publishers) Limited
35 Bedford Row, London WC1R 4JH

ISBN 0-7136-3625-4

© 1994 A & C Black (Publishers) Limited

Filmset by Rowland Phototypesetting Limited,
Bury St Edmunds, Suffolk
Printed in Great Britain by
Cambus Litho, East Kilbride.

About this book

In this book, there are detailed instructions to help you make ships, cranes, a lighthouse and many other working models. The ships are made of cardboard, so don't try sailing them on water. Instead, use aluminium foil to imitate the sea. If you make all the models, you can put them together to create a complete working harbour. Use the cranes to load the ships, and let the ships sail into port by the light of the lighthouse. You could even have a paddle steamer race!

Before you begin take time to read the instructions for the models carefully. Look at the illustrations, too, before you set to work. Some of the models will take time to make, so don't try to do everything in one go.

On page 5 there's a list of things you will need. It's a good idea to have two large boxes to put everything in – one for all your materials and one for your tools. Most of the materials you will need are things you can find around the house; things which would normally be thrown away. Large boxes and cardboard tubes are often thrown away by shops. The larger your selection of boxes, the more varied and interesting your models will be, so start collecting.

You will need to buy some materials, such as PVA glue and wire. But you can save money by sharing these and your tools with friends.

I hope you'll have fun making and using these models. Why not try inventing and making some models of your own?

Can I be the cabin boy?

I want to work the crane.

Here's the cargo.

Where's the ship?

Glossary

This glossary explains some of the words used in the book and describes the various parts used in making the models. All words in the glossary appear in the text in **bold** type.

Axle   a length of wire which connects wheels and **pulleys**.

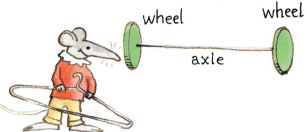

Boom   a long pole or beam fixed at one end and used to help·raise and lower a load.

Bow   the front part of a ship.

Bridge   the high platform over the deck of a ship.

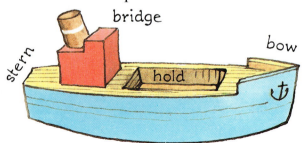

Cogwheel   a wheel with teeth round the edge.

Gantry   a long frame supporting a travelling crane or weight.

Hold   the part of a ship, usually below the deck, where cargo is stored.

Pulley   a wheel for a rope to run over, used for turning and lifting.

Rowlock   pins of wood or metal to support the oars of a rowing boat.

Stern   the back of a ship.

Washer   a bead or metal disc threaded on an **axle** to reduce the friction of moving parts.

Winch   a device for pulling or lifting things by means of a rope wound round a cylinder.

Tools, equipment . . .

awl for making holes
block of wood
brushes
compasses
craft knives
drawing pins
hacksaw
knitting needle
metal ruler

nails
needle
newspaper to work on
paper fasteners
paperclips and pegs
pins
pliers
PVA glue
school glue

scissors
sponge for putting on paint
stapler
torch batteries (1.5V)
torch bulb (4.5V, 3A)
vice
watercolour paints
white emulsion paint
wire cutters

and materials

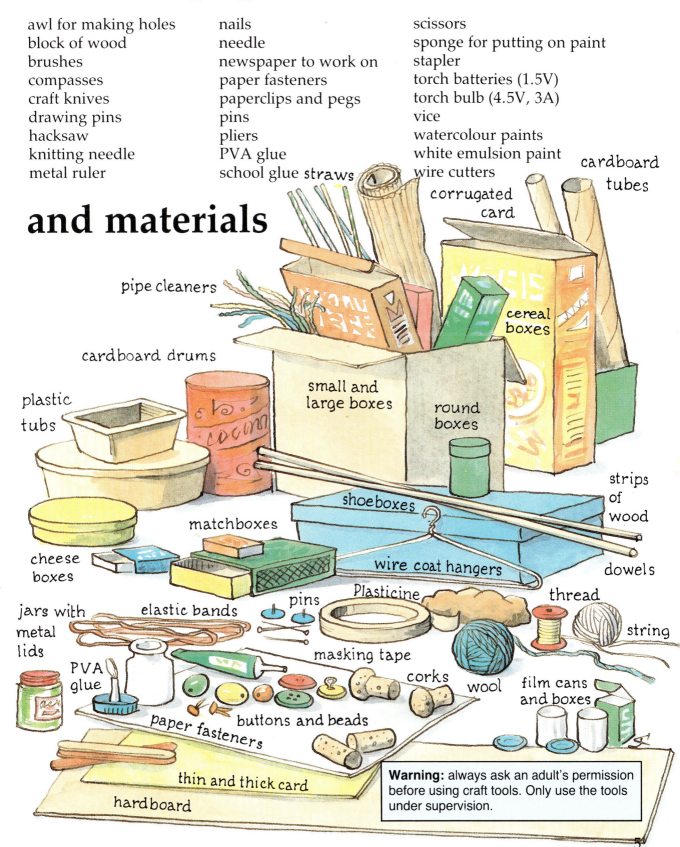

straws

corrugated card

cardboard tubes

pipe cleaners

cereal boxes

cardboard drums

plastic tubs

small and large boxes

round boxes

strips of wood

shoeboxes

cheese boxes

matchboxes

wire coat hangers

dowels

jars with metal lids

elastic bands

pins

Plasticine

thread

string

PVA glue

masking tape

corks

wool

film cans and boxes

paper fasteners

buttons and beads

thin and thick card

hardboard

Warning: always ask an adult's permission before using craft tools. Only use the tools under supervision.

Useful tips

Before you begin, read these pages carefully. They will tell you which tools to use for which jobs, and how to use them safely.

Cutting

Where possible, use scissors to cut card and boxes. The best sort of scissors have rounded ends. Never point scissors at anyone.

If you want to use a craft knife, ask an adult. Make sure the knife is sharp. Protect your work surface by cutting on to a piece of card on top of a thick pad of newspaper.

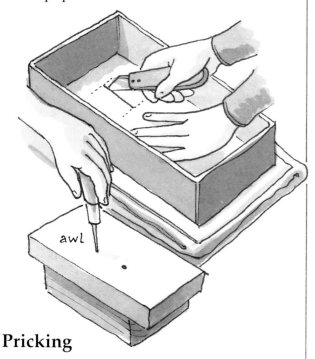

Pricking

If you are using an awl to prick holes in a box, or cutting a box with a knife, put a block of wood inside the box so you've got a hard surface to press down on.

Sawing

Wood or thick cardboard tubing should be held securely in a vice and cut with a hacksaw. Keep your fingers clear of the saw.

Bending card

If you want to bend a piece of card, it's best to score the card first. Place the edge of a metal ruler along the line where you want to bend the card. Press down firmly, and run the blunt point of a knitting needle down the card, following the edge of the ruler.

Bend the card along the score line.

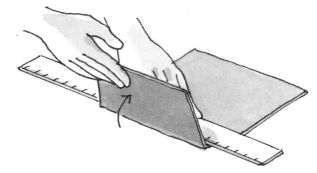

Gluing

Use small pegs or paperclips to hold glued pieces of card together. Then you can get on with something else while the glue is drying.

To join boxes, glue the surfaces together and tape the joins with masking tape. The models can be made stronger and are easier to decorate if you paste paper over all the surfaces first.

To join pieces of card, glue the surfaces together and staple the edges.

To attach a strip of corrugated card round a cheese box, glue the surfaces together. Hold the card in place with an elastic band.

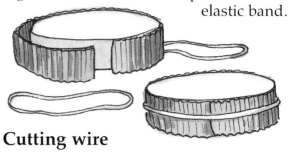

Cutting wire

Cut thin wire with pliers.

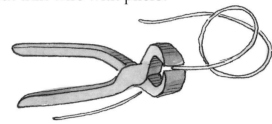

Thick wire should be held securely in a vice and cut with a hacksaw. Keep your fingers clear of the saw.

Make hooks and handles by bending thin wire with pliers.

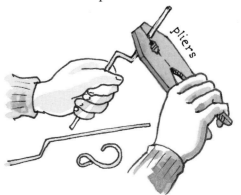

Turning and lifting

It's getting dark, so the captain of this paddle steamer is glad of the lighthouse to guide him into harbour. On the harbour wall a crane with a lifting **boom** swings round to load the paddle steamer.

Welcome home, Dad.

At the end of the **boom** is a string with a hook to lift the load. The string which lifts the **boom** passes down through the tower, and is wound round a wire with handles which acts as a **winch**.

Instructions for making these models can be found on the next six pages.

9

A lifting boom crane

You will need: a shoebox and lid, a cardboard drum (cornflour, cocoa or custard powder), about 14 × 10cm, a small round cheesebox, 3 boxes (box 1 is a strong square box about 12 × 12 × 7cm, boxes 2 and 3 are small cereal boxes about 12 × 7 × 4cm), a 20cm length of strong wire, 2 lengths of string 30cm and 50cm, corrugated card, 2 large-headed nails, two 7cm lengths of soft wire, Plasticine, 2 beads, a wire hook and used matchsticks.

1 Glue card inside the bottom of the shoebox for extra strength.

2 To make the **boom**, make two cuts across the lid of the shoebox. Fold the card along the dotted lines and glue the two pieces together. Strengthen the joins with tape.

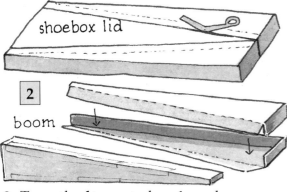

3 Tape the **boom** to box 1 as shown. Tape below the join as well to make a simple hinge.

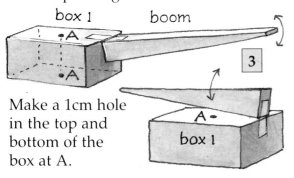

Make a 1cm hole in the top and bottom of the box at A.

4 Glue and tape box 2 to the top of box 1 in the position shown.

5 Put a lump of Plasticine in box 3 and glue and tape it to the side of box 1. The weight of the Plasticine will balance the weight of the **boom**.

6 Make two loops of soft wire as shown. Attach one loop to the **boom** at B by taping the ends of the loop firmly to the **boom**. Attach the second loop to box 2 at C in the same way.

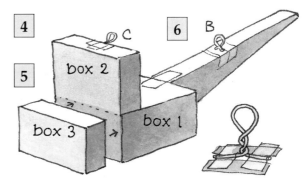

7 Take the lid off the cardboard drum. Use an awl to make holes in opposite sides of the drum at D and in the base of the drum at E.

8 Push the 20cm length of wire through the holes in the drum at D and thread a bead on to each end as a **washer**. Make two right-angled bends in each end of the wire to make handles.

cardboard drum

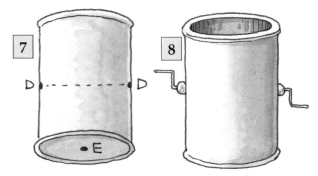

10

9 Make a hole in the centre of the top and bottom of the cheesebox.

10 To make the **cogwheels**, glue a 2cm strip of corrugated card around the cheesebox and the base of the drum. Cut some used matches in half and glue them into the holes in the card to strengthen the teeth of the **cogwheels**.

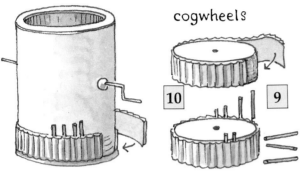

cogwheels

11 Tie one end of the 50cm length of string to the wire running through the inside of the drum. Tape the string firmly in place.

12 Thread the string through the hole in the bottom and top of box 1. Glue and tape box 1 to the drum.

13 Thread the string through the wire loop at C and tie it firmly to the loop at B.

14 Tape one end of the 30cm length of string to the tip of the **boom**. Attach the wire hook to the other end.

15 Mark a point in the centre of the base of the shoebox, about 10cm from one end. Carefully push one of the large-headed nails up through the upside-down shoebox at this point. Tape the head of the nail securely inside the box.

16 Lower the crane on to the nail so that the nail fits into the bottom hole in the drum at E.

17 Hold the other **cogwheel** close to the base of the drum so that the 'teeth' fit together. Push the second nail through the centre holes in the **cogwheel** and into the shoebox.

Attach a piece of cargo.

This cogwheel turns the crane.

This handle lifts the boom.

A paddle steamer

You will need: 2 shoeboxes with lids, 2 round cheeseboxes, 2 strips of corrugated card, a 30cm length of straightened coathanger wire, 2 long elastic bands, used matchsticks, a selection of cardboard boxes and tubes and some card.

1 Cut one shoebox, and its lid, in half. Glue the halves of lid to the bottom of the shoebox halves as shown.

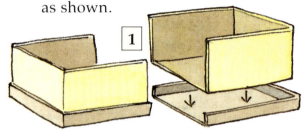

2 Cut each of these shoebox halves down to half its height.

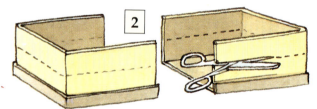

3 Place the second shoebox between the two shoebox halves, as shown. Glue the structure together.

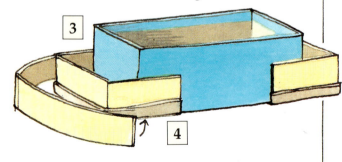

4 Glue the spare pieces of card cut from the top halves of the first shoebox around one end of the structure, to make a pointed **bow** for your paddle steamer.

5 Glue the lid and base of one cheesebox together. Glue a strip of corrugated card around the edge of the box. Make a small hole through the centre of the box.

6 Do the same with the second cheesebox. These cheeseboxes are your paddle steamer's wheels.

7 Thread one of the cheesebox wheels on to the 30cm length of wire. This is the **axle**.

Bend one end of the wire to make a handle. Tape the wire to the cheesebox to hold it in position.

8 Make a hole in each side of the open shoebox at A. The holes should be directly opposite each other.

9 Thread the free end of the wire **axle** through the holes in the box at A. Thread the second cheesebox wheel on to the other end of the wire.

10 Bend the end of the wire and tape it to the cheesebox. The wheels should be slightly lower than the bottom of the shoebox.

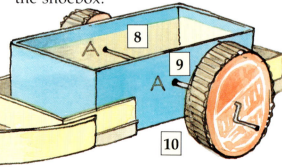

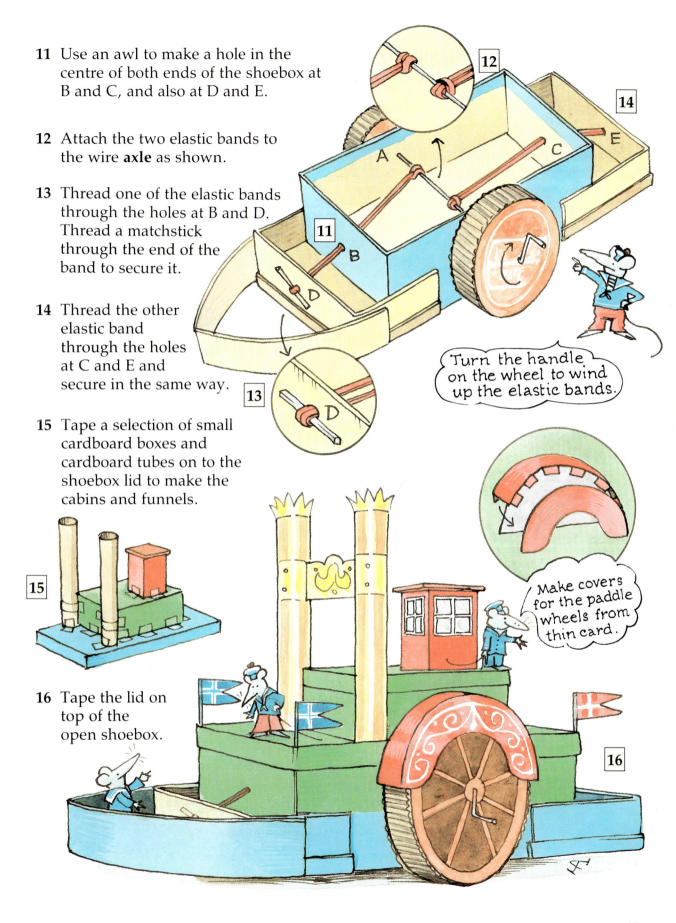

11 Use an awl to make a hole in the centre of both ends of the shoebox at B and C, and also at D and E.

12 Attach the two elastic bands to the wire **axle** as shown.

13 Thread one of the elastic bands through the holes at B and D. Thread a matchstick through the end of the band to secure it.

14 Thread the other elastic band through the holes at C and E and secure in the same way.

15 Tape a selection of small cardboard boxes and cardboard tubes on to the shoebox lid to make the cabins and funnels.

16 Tape the lid on top of the open shoebox.

Turn the handle on the wheel to wind up the elastic bands.

Make covers for the paddle wheels from thin card.

A working lighthouse

You will need: three 1.5V torch batteries, 2 pieces of corrugated card 15 × 15cm, a 40cm length of covered lighting flex, a small jar with a metal lid (a baby food or fish paste jar will be ideal), a cardboard tube into which the jar lid will fit, cut to measure 20cm long, a plastic margarine or ice-cream tub with lid, aluminium foil, tissue paper and a 4.5V–3A torch bulb.

1 Wrap the three torch batteries in one piece of corrugated card, with the corrugations on the outside. Tape it at the ends and middle.

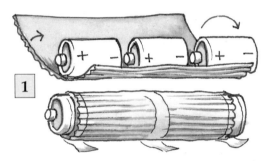

2 Tape the lighting flex to the outside. Wrap the other piece of corrugated card, with the corrugations on the inside, and secure with tape.

3 Ask an adult to expose the wires at each free end of the flex.

4 Push the wrapped batteries into the tube so that the top of the third battery sticks out slightly at the bottom.

5 Cut a round hole in the base of the tub, large enough for the cardboard tube to fit into.

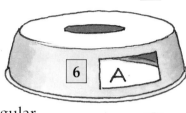

6 Cut a rectangular hole in the side of the tub at A.

7 Slide the cardboard tube through the hole in the base of the tub as shown.

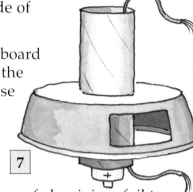

8 Crumple a piece of aluminium foil to make a small mound with a tail as shown. Tape the mound to the centre of the inside of the plastic lid.

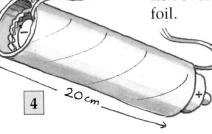

9 Place the cardboard tube over the mound of foil. The top of the third battery should sink into the foil. Position the free end of flex over the foil.

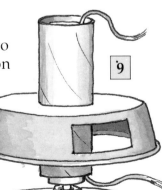

14

10 Slide the plastic tub down over the cardboard tube until it clicks into the lid. The hole in the side of the tub should be positioned beside the tail of aluminium foil and the free end of flex. Feed the flex out through the hole. Tape the tube to the tub at B.

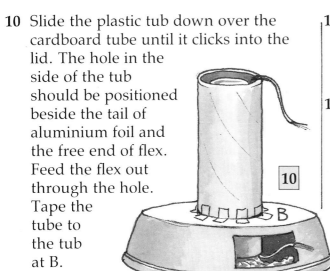

11 Use an awl to make a hole in the centre of the jar lid. The hole should be large enough to take the screw base of the torch bulb. Make two smaller holes in the lid at C.

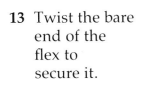

12 Holding the jam jar lid upside down, thread the free end of flex at the top of the tube, through one small hole, across the top of the lid, and down through the second small hole.

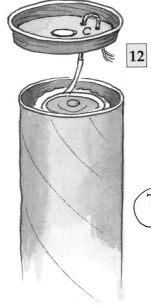

13 Twist the bare end of the flex to secure it.

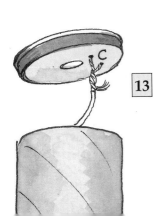

14 Push the jar lid a little way into the cardboard tube so that it rests on top of the first battery.

15 Screw the torch bulb into the centre hole in the jar lid. The base of the bulb should touch the base of the first battery.

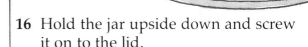

16 Hold the jar upside down and screw it on to the lid.

Glue crumpled tissue paper round the base of the tube. Paint it to look like rocks.

Finish the top with a lid.

Touch the flex on the foil to light the bulb.

Winches and pulleys

Cranes are used to lift loads. The cargo ship on this page has its own crane to lift the cargo on to the jetty. Waiting on the jetty is another crane.

All cranes need to be balanced so that they don't tip over. This crane has a **gantry**. A string with a hook runs over a **pulley** at one end of the **gantry** to lift the cargo. A sliding weight is moved along the **gantry** to balance the crane as the cargo is raised and lowered.

A cargo ship

You will need: 2 identical cereal boxes, a small square plastic margarine tub, 3 small cardboard boxes, a cardboard tube, 20cm of thin wire, 34cm of strong, thick wire, strong card, a sweet tube, 4 corks, a small elastic band and 30cm of string.

1 Cut the long flaps from one end of each cereal box.

2 Mark points halfway along the sides and halfway along the open ends of box 1. Join the points as shown and cut along the lines. Do the same on the bottom of the box.

3 Tuck in the sides and tape the end flaps together as a point. Then tape the cut edges together.

4 Glue the cut-off long flaps around the top edge as a guard rail. This is the **bow** of your ship.

5 Mark points halfway along the sides of box 2 as before, but this time mark points on the open end to divide it into thirds. Join the points as shown and cut along the lines. Do the same on the bottom of the box.

6 Tuck in the sides and tape the end flaps together. Then tape the cut edges to the sides. You will find that the top and bottom stick out a bit. Fold down the spare piece inside the end flaps and tape the ends flat.

7 Glue the cut-off long flaps around the top edge as a guard rail. This is the **stern** of your ship.

8 Glue and tape the **bow** and **stern** sections together.

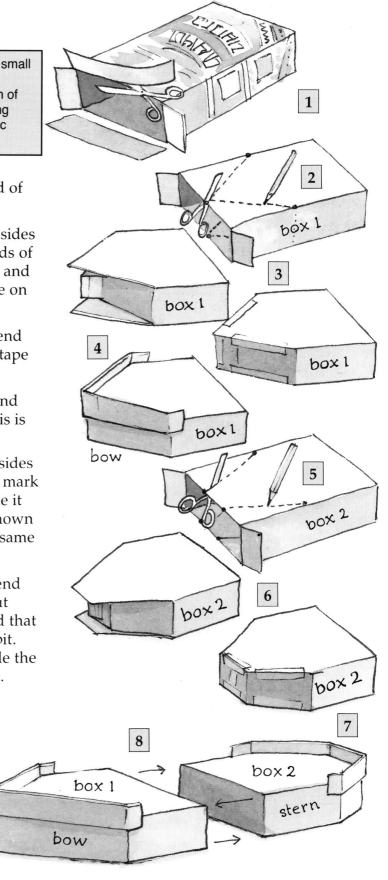

18

9 Cut a hole in the centre of the top of the **bow** section with a craft knife. The hole should be large enough for the margarine tub to sit inside. Glue the margarine tub into position in the hole. This margarine tub is the ship's cargo **hold**.

10 Glue and tape the three remaining boxes together to make the ship's **bridge**. The box nearest the **hold**, box 3, must have a flap lid. Add a cardboard tube funnel.

11 Cut a small piece out of the front of box 3, as shown.

12 Glue the box and tube structure to the **stern** section of the ship.

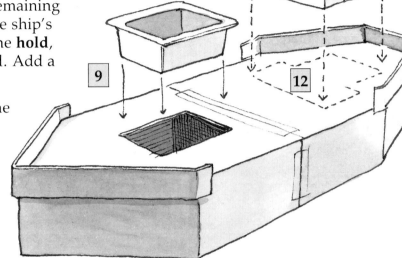

13 Make a small hole in each side of box 3 at A. Thread a 20cm length of wire through the holes.

14 Bend one end of the wire to make a handle.

15 Tie a 30cm length of string around the wire at B. Hold the free end of string clear of the box and close the lid.

16 Cut the sweet tube in half, to make two pillars. Glue a cork into each end of each pillar.

17 Push a 5cm length of thin wire into the end of each cork.

18 Bend the 34cm length of wire in half. Bend the folded end of the wire at C.

Turn the page for more instructions.

19 Push the free ends of the folded wire into the cork on top of one of the pillars at D. This wire is the crane.

20 Make a hole through the middle of the other pillar at E.

21 Make two holes at F just in front of the **bridge**, and push the two pillars into these holes.

22 Drop the small elastic band over the crane pillar. Push a 10cm piece of wire through the hole at E in the other pillar, through this elastic band and into the **bridge** at G. Bend the free end of wire into a handle. The elastic band should be tight when the pillars are upright.

23 Cut a piece of card the same length as the **bridge** but three times as wide. Make two holes in this card to fit the top wires of the pillars.

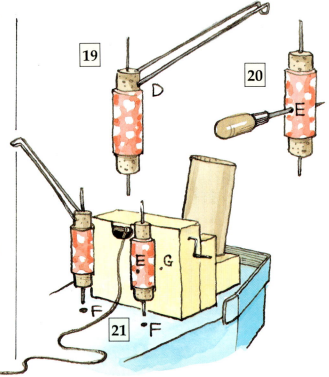

24 Push the card on to the wires and glue it to the top of the **bridge**.

25 Thread the end of the string between the pillars and over the bent end of the crane. Fix a hook to the end for the cargo.

By turning the handles you can swing the crane round and lift the cargo from the **hold** on to the jetty.

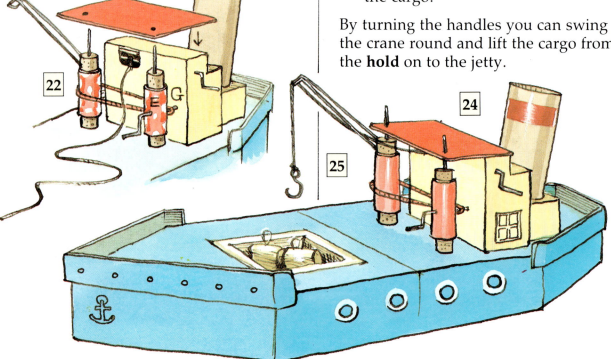

A swinging gantry crane

You will need: a 30cm length of dowel, a large and small matchbox, 2 wire coathangers, 3 corks, Plasticine, two 15cm straightened lengths of coathanger wire, a bead, string, 4 boxes (box 1 is about 18 × 12 × 9cm, box 2 is about 22 × 12 × 5cm, boxes 3 and 4 are about 8 × 7 × 2cm), an elastic band about 8cm long, card, paperclips, 6 film can lids, about 5cm of thin wire and nine 2.5cm thin nails.

1 Make a hole with an awl in the tray of the large matchbox at A. Push the dowel through the hole and glue and tape it in position.

2 Slide the matchbox sleeve over the tray. Tape a coathanger to each side of the matchbox as shown. Tape all round the matchbox, to hold the coathangers firmly in place.

3 Tape a cork between the two coathangers at B and C. Push two nails into one of the corks at D.

4 Tap a nail into the end of the dowel. Carefully cut off the head.

5 Make a small **pulley** by gluing two discs of card to the ends of a cork.

6 Bend one end of a 15cm length of wire to make a handle. Thread on the bead as a **washer** and push the wire through the matchbox at E. Push on the **pulley**, bend the end of the wire and tape it to the **pulley** to make a **winch**.

7 Tie an 80cm length of string to the **pulley**. Run the string over the cork at D between the pins as shown.

8 Tie a hook made from a piece of wire to the free end of the string.

Turn over the page for more instructions.

21

9 Straighten one end of two paperclips.

10 Make four holes at F in the small matchbox cover.

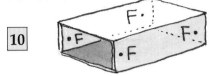

11 Push a lump of Plasticine into the box. Thread the paperclips through the holes in the box at F.

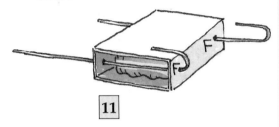

12 Position the box between the wire coathangers, with the bent ends of the paperclips over one wire. Bend the other ends of the paperclips over the other wire. Wrap the matchbox with tape. You have now made the swinging **gantry** with the hook and a sliding counterweight.

The box should slide along the wire.

13 To make the base of the crane, cut two sections out of box 1, as shown. Make a hole in the top of the box, wide enough for the dowel.

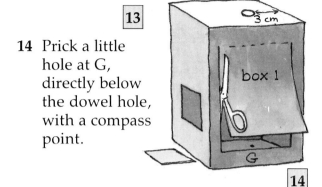

3 cm

box 1

14 Prick a little hole at G, directly below the dowel hole, with a compass point.

G

15 Tape and glue box 1 on to box 2.

16 Position the two small boxes, 3 and 4, as shown, each side of the small square hole in box 1. Glue and tape them in place.

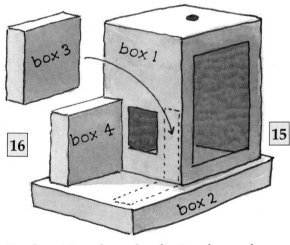

box 3

box 1

box 4

box 2

17 Push a 15cm length of wire through the centre of one small box at H, then thread it through the elastic band and push it through the other small box at H.

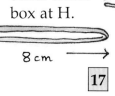

8 cm

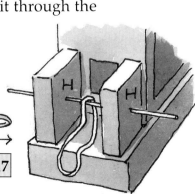

H   H

18 Bend the ends of the wire to make two handles.

19 Poke the elastic band through the small square hole into box 1.

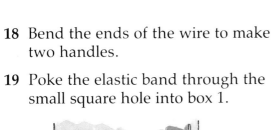

20 To fit the swinging **gantry** into the base, lower the dowel through the hole in box 1. Thread it through the elastic band and poke the headless nail into the little hole at G.

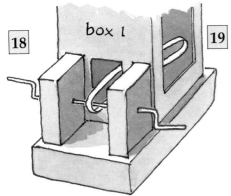

This handle turns the gantry.

This handle lifts the cargo.

21 Use an awl to make a hole through the centre of six film can lids. Push a nail through each hole. Fasten three of these lids to each long side of box 2 as wheels.

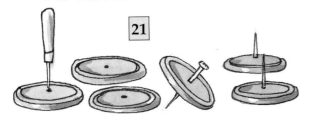

22 Attach a piece of cargo (see page 31) to the hook. Turn the handles at H to make the crane swivel. Turn the handle at E to lift the cargo up and lower it. If the cargo is very heavy, there is a danger of the crane tipping over. To prevent this, slide the counterweight back to balance the load.

The jetty

You will need: 2 shoeboxes, strong card or hardboard about 100 × 15cm, two 100cm strips of wood, 2 corks, 4 jelly boxes, two 20cm lengths of wire, thin wire for hooks and two 70cm lengths of strong thread.

1 Glue the strips of wood, 9cm apart, down the length of the card, to form tracks for the truck and crane.

2 Position the two shoeboxes, upside-down and lengthways, underneath each end of the track. Glue them in place. This is the jetty.

3 Glue two jelly boxes inside the tracks at each end of the jetty as shown.

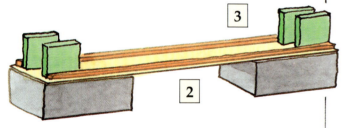

4 To make a **winch**, first bend one end of a 20cm length of wire to make a handle. Push the other end through the side of one of the jelly boxes at A. Then push it through a cork (if the cork is not tight on the wire, poke in matches and glue), and out through the jelly box on the other side. Make the other **winch** in the same way.

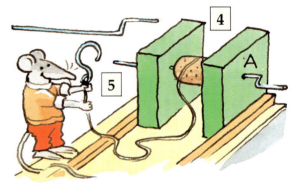

5 Tie a 70cm length of thread to each cork, and tie a wire hook to the end of each thread.

The tipper truck

You will need: a small cereal box, a small rectangular butter tub, 2 paper fasteners, 2 corks and strong card.

1 Cut two pieces of strong card, as shown. Glue them to each end of the cereal box. Pierce holes at A.

2 Fix the butter tub between the tops of the pieces of card with paper fasteners. The tub should be free to tilt to each side.

3 Glue four pieces of cork under the box as wheels, so that they just fit inside the tracks.

Fix hooks of bent wire to each end.

A rowing boat

You will need: a small cereal box, a cork, card and 4 used matchsticks.

1 Tape up all open edges of the box.

2 Mark points halfway along each end at A. Join A to A with a pencil line.

3 Measure the distance between A and B. Measure this same distance on the central line to find point C. Join B to C. Do the same at the other end of the box.

4 Do the same on the bottom of the box.

5 Cut along all these lines.

6 Glue the top side flaps down.

7 Squeeze one end out to a point, so that the triangles ABC overlap. Glue them together. Do the same at the other end to make a boat with sharp ends.

8 The box is now narrower and the bottom side flaps will overlap. Glue them together and glue the bottom of the boat to another piece of card.

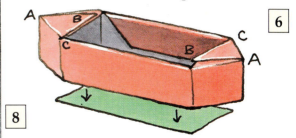

9 Glue a cork inside the box as a seat.

10 Glue used matchsticks to the edges of the boat, to make **rowlocks**.

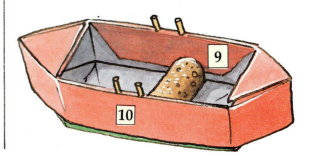

A lifting bridge

Where a road crosses a canal or the entrance to a harbour, some sort of bridge has to be made. It's not always possible to build a bridge high enough to clear the tallest ships so the traffic is stopped and the road swings or lifts to allow the ships to pass through.

Here are instructions to help you make a lifting bridge for your harbour.

You will need: 2 shoeboxes with lids, paper fasteners, a piece of wood or thick card for a base, 2 toilet roll tubes, straightened lengths of coathanger wire, corks, thread, pins, used matchsticks, scraps of card and 2 small matchboxes.

1 Cut one of the shoebox lids in half widthways. Cut away a strip 2cm deep from the top of each half and make holes, as shown.

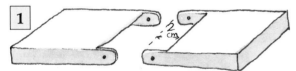

2 Hold one of the lid halves in the position shown. Fix it to the upside-down shoebox with paper fasteners at A.

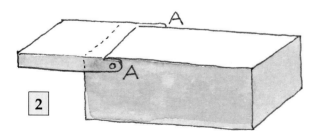

3 Attach the second shoebox lid half to the second shoebox, in exactly the same way.

4 To make the **winch** towers, cut two flaps in the bottom of each toilet roll tube as shown. Fold back the flaps.

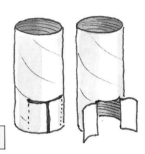

5 Cut a small triangle out of the top of each tower at B. Make holes on both sides of the tower at C with a compass point.

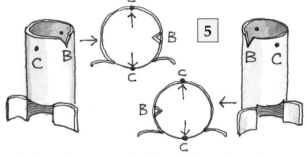

6 Bend one end of two 10cm lengths of wire to make two handles.

7 Push one piece of wire through the holes at C in each of the two towers. Push a piece of cork on the end of each wire.

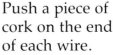

26

8 Position the boxes so that the two halves of the bridge meet. Glue and tape the two shoeboxes to the base.

9 Glue one **winch** tower to the side of one shoebox at D. Glue the second **winch** tower to the other shoebox at E.

11 Add a small matchbox to the top of each **winch** tower, to make control towers.

12 Make traffic control signals with red and green drawing pins pushed into two corks. Fix them to the control towers with long pins.

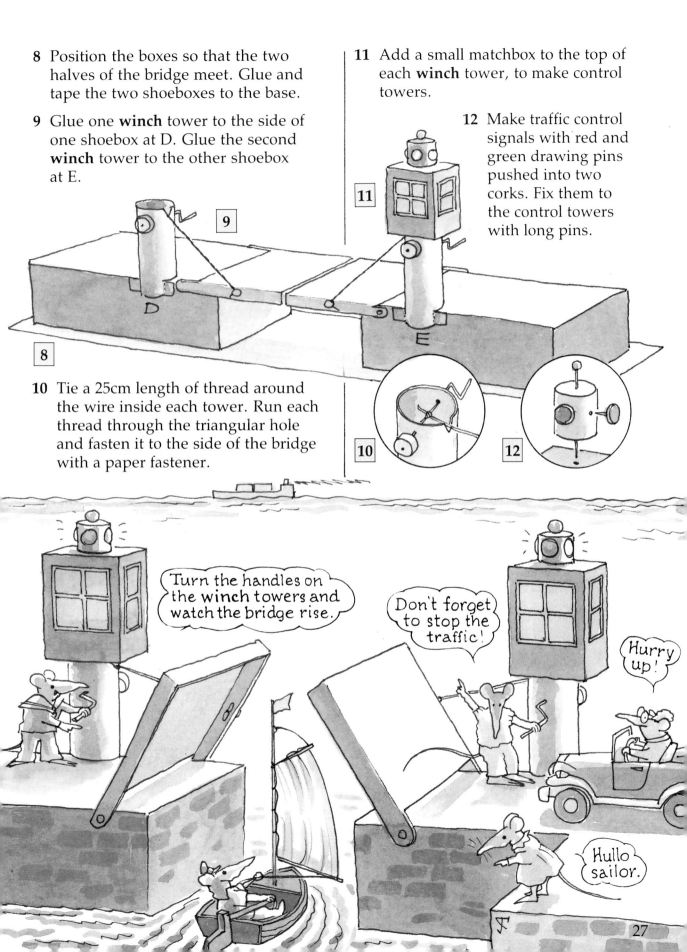

10 Tie a 25cm length of thread around the wire inside each tower. Run each thread through the triangular hole and fasten it to the side of the bridge with a paper fastener.

Turn the handles on the **winch** towers and watch the bridge rise.

Don't forget to stop the traffic!

Hurry up!

Hullo sailor.

Warehouses

You can make many different buildings which, when arranged together, will form a complete dockyard and harbour area. Tape each building to an upside-down shoebox base.

Here are instructions for an upright warehouse with three floors. To make a long warehouse, cut the lid in half lengthways, and use one half for a floor and one half for a roof.

> You will need: a shoebox with a lid, 3 small matchboxes, a cork, about 20cm of thin wire, a used matchstick and about 30cm of thin string or thread.

1 Mark two lines on the inside of the box to divide the house into three equal floors. Make two 3cm cuts in each side of the box at A and B.

2 Draw in the thick black lines and the dotted lines in the positions shown.

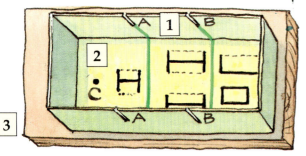

3 Put the box on a block of wood and cut along the thick black lines. Fold along the dotted lines to make the windows and the door. Make a hole at C with an awl.

4 Cut the shoebox lid into three equal sections as shown.

5 Use the centre section of the cut lid to make a roof for the building.

6 Use the two end sections of the cut lid to make floors for the inside of the house.

7 Cut a slot halfway along the edge of each lid section.

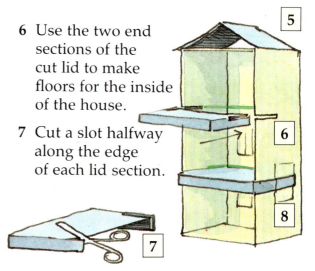

8 Slide the cut lid sections into the floor slits. Glue and tape in position.

9 Push the cork on to a 12cm length of thin wire.

10 To make a **winch**, thread a small matchbox on to each end of the wire. Bend one end of the wire to make a handle.

11 Tie one end of the string around the cork on the **winch**.

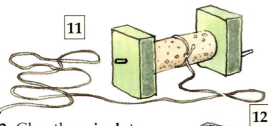

12 Glue the **winch** to the inside of the house, on the top floor. Thread the string through the hole at C.

13 Cut the sides of the third matchbox cover as shown.

14 Fold in the small piece and glue it to the sides. Make holes at D.

15 Push the used matchstick through the matchbox at D to make a **pulley**.

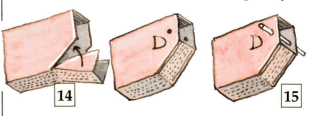

16 Glue and tape the matchbox to the outside of the house, over the hole at C. Thread the **winch** string over the matchstick.

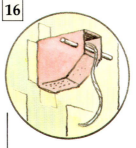

17 Make a small hook out of some thin wire and attach it to the other end of the string.

People

Use pipe cleaners, corks and egg boxes to make little people to add to your models. Here are some ideas to help you.

Pipe cleaner figures

1 Make a figure by twisting two pipe cleaners together.

2 Sew or glue on a covered button for the head. Draw on a face with felt pens. Sew or glue on wool for hair.

3 Make clothes from pieces of felt.

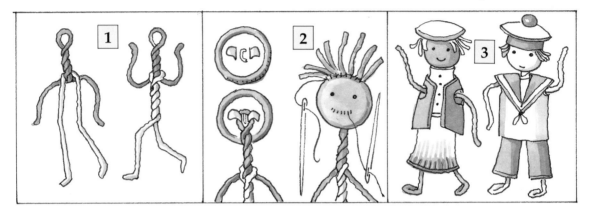

Cork figures

1 Use corks of different shapes and sizes to make bodies and heads. Join the corks together with pins or glue.

2 Use pipe cleaners or wire for arms.

3 Use bottle tops for hats. Cut clothes from tissue paper, and glue these on to the cork bodies.

Egg-box figures

1 Cut out a piece of egg-box for the body. Glue on a bead for the head.

2 Use pipe cleaners or wire for arms.

3 Make clothes from felt and tissue paper.

Cargo

Use small boxes, corks, lolly sticks and net fruit bags to make cargo for your harbour. Here are some ideas to help you.

1 Cover small sweet boxes or other similar small boxes with paper.

2 Glue them together to form parcels.

3 Paint a small box to look like a container.

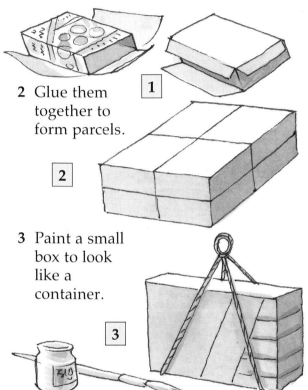

4 Paint corks to make them look like barrels. Tie them together with string.

5 Glue string around each cargo parcel. Shape the top of the string into a ring. The rings will easily fit over the hooks on your **winches** and cranes.

6 Use net bags to hold boxes or barrels.

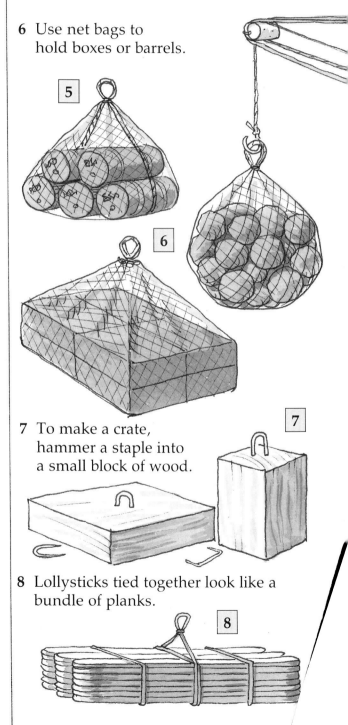

7 To make a crate, hammer a staple into a small block of wood.

8 Lollysticks tied together look like a bundle of planks.

Decorating your models

Decorating is easier if you paint all over the models with emulsion paint first. If the surfaces are waxy, or if there are many taped joins, paste paper all over a model before painting. As well as making any joined pieces stronger, this also makes painting easier.

Cut and glue pieces of coloured paper to make flags and other decorations for the ships and buildings.

Details of windows and portholes can be painted or drawn on with pens. But if you have sticky-backed labels, such as jam jar labels, you can draw the details on to the labels, cut out your illustration and then stick them on to your models.

Make railings for the ships and the harbour from used matchsticks. Link the matchsticks with thread.